W9-BXY-874

PLANT POWER
MEAT-EATING PLANTS

by Mari Schuh

Ideas for Parents and Teachers

Pogo Books let children practice reading informational text while introducing them to nonfiction features such as headings, labels, sidebars, maps, and diagrams, as well as a table of contents, glossary, and index.

Carefully leveled text with a strong photo match offers early fluent readers the support they need to succeed.

Before Reading

- "Walk" through the book and point out the various nonfiction features. Ask the student what purpose each feature serves.
- Look at the glossary together. Read and discuss the words.

Read the Book

- Have the child read the book independently.
- Invite him or her to list questions that arise from reading.

After Reading

- Discuss the child's questions. Talk about how he or she might find answers to those questions.
- Prompt the child to think more. Ask: Did you know about meat-eating plants before you read this book? What more would you like to learn after reading it?

Pogo Books are published by Jump!
5357 Penn Avenue South
Minneapolis, MN 55419
www.jumplibrary.com

Library of Congress Cataloging-in-Publication Data

Names: Schuh, Mari C., 1975- author.
Title: Meat-eating plants / by Mari Schuh.
Description: Minneapolis, MN : Jump!, Inc., [2018]
Series: Plant power
Audience: Ages 7-10. | Includes index.
Identifiers: LCCN 2017052361 (print)
LCCN 2017053380 (ebook)
ISBN 9781624968792 (ebook)
ISBN 9781624968778 (hardcover : alk. paper)
ISBN 9781624968785 (pbk.)
Subjects: LCSH: Carnivorous plants—Juvenile literature.
Classification: LCC QK917 (ebook)
LCC QK917 .S38 2019 (print) | DDC 581.6—dc23
LC record available at https://lccn.loc.gov/2017052361

Editor: Jenna Trnka
Book Designer: Molly Ballanger

Photo Credits: Cathy Keifer/Shutterstock, cover, 11; Trent Townsend/Shutterstock, 1; Kuttelvaserova Stuchelova/Shutterstock, 3; irin-k/Shutterstock, 4 (wasp); Ed Reschke/SuperStock, 4 (plant); Ed Reschke/Getty, 5; Egon Zitter/Shutterstock, 6-7; blickwinkel/Alamy, 8-9; Marco Uliana/Shutterstock, 10; Sergei Aleshin/Shutterstock, 12-13; Paul Starosta/Getty, 14-15, 16, 17; inga spence/Alamy, 18-19, 20-21; Only Fabrizio/Shutterstock, 23.

Printed in the United States of America at Corporate Graphics in North Mankato, Minnesota.

TABLE OF CONTENTS

CHAPTER 1

LURING PREY

A wasp lands on a colorful pitcher plant. The insect eats the plant's sweet, gooey **nectar**.

Wait! It's a trap! The wasp slides down the plant's long tube. It lands in the pitcher. It drowns in the pool below. The wasp becomes the plant's tasty meal.

Pitcher plants are meat-eating plants. They are death traps. They lure in **prey**. How? With sweet nectar. Insects climb inside the plant. They quickly fall down the plant's smooth, slippery sides. **Enzymes** and **acids** then **dissolve** the prey. They become a soupy meal for the hungry plant.

DID YOU KNOW?

Meat-eating plants usually live in wet areas. These include **bogs** and sandy swamps. These areas do not have many **nutrients**. These killer plants eat bugs and other animals to get nutrients.

pitcher ····▶

window

cobra lily

Cobra lilies look like cobra snakes. And they are ready to attack. The smell of nectar lures prey into this sneaky plant. Clear areas on the top of the plant look like tiny windows. They confuse the prey. They think they can get out. But they are trapped.

DID YOU KNOW?

There are more than 600 kinds of meat-eating plants. They eat all sorts of insects. Ants, beetles, and grasshoppers. Some even eat frogs, lizards, and birds!

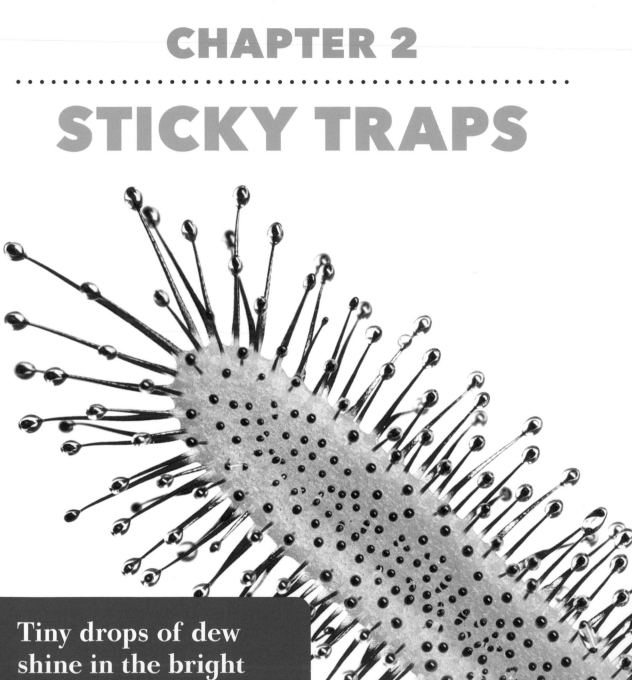

CHAPTER 2

STICKY TRAPS

Tiny drops of dew shine in the bright sun on sundew plants.

Wrong! The shiny drops on the ends of the plant's hairs are not what they seem. They are sticky, gluey traps. Watch out! Insects and other thirsty prey try to drink the drops of dew. But they get stuck.

The more they wiggle, the more stuck they get. Sticky leaves bend and fold around the prey. Then enzymes get to work. They help the sundew **digest** its tasty meal. The plant's leaves unfold. Beware! It is ready to trap again!

DID YOU KNOW?

Some tiny sundew plants are very small. They are about the size of a quarter.

Butterworts look harmless. But they use their sticky, greasy leaves to catch tiny prey. Prey lands on the leaves. Then the plant makes more sticky goo. The unlucky visitor is trapped. Num!

CHAPTER 3

Is life safer for underwater insects? No! The waterwheel plant floats just below the water's surface.

bristles

Long, pointed **bristles** on each leaf feel for prey. The traps snap shut in the blink of an eye.

Venus flytrap leaves look like tiny taco shells. But they have something extra. Long, sharp teeth! Beetles and other bugs smell the plant's sweet nectar. They are attracted to its bright red color. But when they touch the plant's tiny hairs, they are doomed. Snap!

TAKE A LOOK!

Venus flytraps have tiny trigger hairs on their inner lobes. These lobes can snap shut in less than one second. They do this if an insect brushes against more than one of the hairs. The teeth trap the insect inside. **Glands** release juices that then help the plant digest the insect.

TEETH

LOBE

TRIGGER HAIR

Meat-eating plants feed themselves. Most of them cannot move, so they appeal to their prey to come to them. Then they use their powers to trap and eat insects! What will they eat next?

ACTIVITIES & TOOLS

TRY THIS!

DIGESTING FOOD

See how meat-eating plants break down food in this simple activity.

What You Need:
- one egg
- antacid tablets
- vinegar
- two glasses
- clock, watch, or timer

1. **Fill two short glasses with vinegar. The vinegar acts as the enzymes meat-eating plants use to break down prey.**

2. **Add a few antacid tablets to one glass.**

3. **Add an egg to the other glass. The egg and antacid tablets are like the prey that get trapped in meat-eating plants.**

4. **After one hour, look at the glasses. Have the tablets and egg changed in any way? How do they look?**

5. **After three more hours, look at the glasses again.**

6. **The next morning, look at the glasses. Note what has happened. This is much like what happens to prey caught in meat-eating plants.**

GLOSSARY

acids: Liquids that can break down food.

bogs: Areas with soft, wet land.

bristles: Short, stiff hairs on plants and animals.

digest: To turn food into nutrients that a plant, animal, or person can use.

dissolve: To disappear when mixed with liquid.

enzymes: Proteins that help digest food.

glands: Organs that produce natural chemicals.

nectar: A sweet liquid found in many flowers.

nutrients: Proteins, minerals, and other substances plants need to grow and live.

prey: An animal that is hunted by another animal or eaten by a plant for food.

INDEX

TO LEARN MORE

Learning more is as easy as 1, 2, 3.

1) **Go to www.factsurfer.com**

2) **Enter "meateatingplants" into the search box.**

3) **Click the "Surf" button to see a list of websites.**

With factsurfer, finding more information is just a click away.